Management Development for Care & Nursing Home Managers

Equipping Home Managers to raise Care and Quality standards.

Liam Palmer

ISBN: 978-1-326-63312-7

PublishNation
www.publishnation.co.uk

Dedicated to Heather Palmer

Introduction to "Management Development for Care & Nursing Home Managers"

There is a revolution going in social care – like two tectonic plates touching – with dramatically raised expectations and a social care model still influenced by hospital practices from 50 years ago. When you add in the dramatic expansion of care homes in the next 20 years set against so many home managers retiring in the next 10 years..we have a storm coming. Something needs to give. In my view, we need to adapt and we need to prepare;

The adaption of our social care model needs to include;

o   A greater use of IT – integrated and streamlined systems, reporting tools, information gathering. Where possible, we need smart technology to help with giving and co-ordinating care.
o   A rethinking of the team structures and roles to meet these greater expectations.

The preparation for these changes needs to include;

o   A new cohort of skilled home leaders who can balance these opposing forces, we need up-skilled managers who can weather this storm and help the sector transform.
o   Staff engagement and empowerment – a positive management style, incorporating upskilling and informing the team about the wider context of standards, a true team approach.
In short, we need highly effective leader managers and we need high performing, unified teams. It is a call to leadership.

In this book, I will focus on the preparation needed and have drawn together some of the most enlightened thinking available from industry, and other disciplines and weaved it into anecdotes and articles to bring this knowledge into care, to help raise standards, to start some debate on how we can make this transition.

I am very positive about the future of the social care industry. I seek to raise awareness through my writing with most of these articles having been published on a professional network. It has been a valuable experience to learn that home manager peers from around the world (Canada, US, NZ, Aus) are facing many of the same issues

Some individual articles took 4 months, as I worked on stripping out the complexity to find that elusive kernel of truth, the primary thing. Only then was I ready to write. By publishing single articles it has been educational and grounding to get instant feedback. I have received 170 comments – from Carers to Country Managers to Global Clinical Leads and CEOs of large care companies. For all those who read, commented, shared, challenged - sincerely, thank you.

I hope you find value in the articles that follow. Do use the reflective practice after each article, if appropriate. Please share it with nurses, seniors, carers, trainers. Let's pull together. With many minds engaged, grappling with these issues, there is no limit to what we can achieve. Thank you.

Liam Palmer

Birmingham

June 2016

Foreword to "Management Development for Care and Nursing Home Managers."

This book is long awaited, it offers sound ideas and thinking to support home managers and their teams to provide outstanding care and services. Liam speaks from the heart, from his experience as a manager and as a caring individual using a wide range of skills and abilities to get the best for his team. It shows managers how to coach their teams effectively so that they are equipped to deliver outstanding care.

One of the really helpful things about this book is that it highlights some of the issues that arose for Liam, he explains what worked and what didn't, but he learn from both; in the book he explains how he reflected and honed his skills from his practical applications. Liam also explained the academic underpinning behind his decision making; demonstrating how his practical approach had a sound basis.

This is the first book of its kind and really hits the mark, it's pragmatic solutions are useful and thought provoking; well worth spending a few hours with. A must read for care home managers wanting to excel.

Dr Terry Tucker

Distinguished Professor of Healthcare

London

June 2016

Contents

Contents

Part 3 – Masterclass in Leadership Qualities

Part 1 – Masterclass in Management

Part 1 – Masterclass in Management - overview

In this series of articles, we take a new look at some familiar themes and beliefs – firstly looking at seeing a care home manager as the best job in the world and I made my case for this.

We move on to examining the importance of home and having empathy for those in our care. I look at judgements we can all make and how they can be wrong.

I look at a core theme in care at the moment – staff engagement and take a radical view as to why levels are not where they might be.

Next we look at a core belief I came across in care – the "problem staff" and I review this assessment with a twist.

Lastly, for me, delivering great care consistently will always be through the team. What if we don't have an established team – how do you make it established and function? I introduce a model (Myers Briggs) for you to proactively develop your care home team.

1.1 Care Home Manager - best job in the world?

It has been a year since I moved to a private care provider working with older people after working as a senior manager in a large private hospital and 6 months since I took up the reins of a 79 bed residential home. I was equally excited and apprehensive about the move and the possibilities for working in this sector. I had never considered "care" before - my thoughts influenced by a jumble sale in an old people's home as a child, seeing a few people with Alzheimer's in a hospital and then of course the scare stories in the media of neglect and what sounded like a scary place to work.

When I took up the reins of my first home, I saw those suffering with dementia and went to see them every day - for a while my heart sunk, I am a big-hearted person and have a sweet spot for older people but still, the reality and tragedy of their pain and loss hit me hard, I wondered, did I have enough heart to love these people every day, keep pushing for the very best for them? After a few months, these people came alive to me, we started to get to know each other even if no words were shared, we have our jokes, smiles, habits - I became the "young man with the big smile - always smiling" according to several of these lovely older ladies that stay with us. I am happy with that - if my smile gives them happiness, well it is not much, but it is something.

Several precious memories of my work in care over the last year care come from 2 particular residents;

One who told me about her husband of 50 years - "best man I ever met, never a cross word, he made me laugh" she was still praising him years after he passed. She had dementia - was her memory being overly sentimental I wondered? I got to know her a bit - she was a remarkable lady and I think she was telling the truth. What an inspiration - to live in such a way that your wife still praises you after you passed - amazing lady! I hope to visit her in Cambridge next week.

Secondly, a lady in my dementia unit said "You are very handsome and you are lovely, I am not just saying that, I really mean it" she said looking in my eyes. She said that "Your mother must be so proud of you." Whether it is true is irrelevant, at that moment, this lady meant it, said it with such conviction. I could have cried. Nicest thing anyone had ever said to me. A precious moment.

There are times where the risks inherent in the role of care home manager can be pressing, it is by no means a job for the faint-hearted but with a degree of autonomy as registered manager and the help and support of a great staff team, nearly anything is possible.

Care Home Manager - best job in the world? I think so.

1.1 Reflective practice on **Care Home Manager – best job in the world?**

Key themes covered

Person centred care, joy in service, precious moments from those with work with.

What does this article mean to you?

What can / would you apply from this learning to your practice?

Other notes

1.2 "There's no place like home!" (Dorothy, Wizard of Oz) What does home mean to you?

This reflection came after sharing a moment with a lady who lives in the dementia wing of our care home. It got me thinking and if I am really honest, upset me a bit. The link with Dorothy (in the movie above - 1939) will become clear a bit later - bear with me.

As I do one of my daily walks around the home sharing and smiling with those living in this community, this lady would look distressed if I came within 10 feet of her and say "go away – I don't like you." Fair enough, I thought! After, she even tried to hit me a few times in frustration. She would shake my hand initially then pull my arm in till it hurt. Later we agreed for her to try being more gentle. She meant no harm and was simply reaching out for attention in her own way.

More recently, after she had injured her arm, she reached out to hold my hand. I took it. I later checked she was getting her pain relief and made extra checks on her well-being, giving her some reassurance about the wound healing on her arm. She would look at me, hold my hand for 10 seconds or so, feel that care and then let go. It worked and I was happy she felt understood and supported.

I saw her yesterday; her bottom lip was shaking. I bent down and offered my hand. She took both. She was fearful and wanted to go home. She asked how to get home - "I don't know, I don't know" she said, clearly very distressed. It seemed like her heart was breaking. It reminded me of Dorothy in the Wizard of Oz yearning for home. She asked me not to leave. Distressed, she pulled me in. I pulled back slightly, weary of being hit and yet it was a desire to pull me close. I felt embarrassed that I thought to protect myself from a slap and instead it was an embrace! Later when she calmed and I left, I found a female carer to give her more physical reassurance.

The whole episode made me think – how would it feel if I could never go home? This lady had enjoyed her own home for all her life, a garden with complete control and choice and here she was now sharing a living room with many "strangers". Perhaps that what it was for her, a memory of the feeling of home and that if she goes back, everything will be ok.

Whilst I will never know understand her feelings exactly, (this lady is partially verbal), I can take a guess that it was the same need we all have– to have a refuge from the outside world, where we are understood, loved, safe and secure. A place where we are known, of shared memories, familiarity – where we matter. For anybody, needing to give up their home and embracing a care home community is a big step, it often works beautifully, but at best it is a replacement home for the one given up. At times, for that very reason it will fall short of that individual's expectations.

Today, that feeling resonates me. I feel it keenly. What can I do to make this place feel like home for all who live here? We can foster a culture of a close knit, high morale team with a family feel. We can continually strive for high standards and encourage keen observation and personalized care and remind staff that what these people want and need is exactly the same as you and I. I cannot take this lady to her former home but I can strive to give her a feeling of home through my service. In the end, I think we are the same, old and young alike.

That's enough for me today. I am going home.

1.2 Reflective practice on **"There's no place like home!" (Dorothy, Wizard of Oz). What does home mean to you?**

Key themes in this article

The meaning of home as security, comfort especially when afraid. Avoiding judgement. Seeing the person – good practice in dementia care.

What does this article mean to you?

What can / would you apply from this learning to your practice?

Other notes

1.3 Staff engagement / are we missing something?

I have noticed there is now a much greater focus on staff engagement, it seems to have become the elusive "holy grail" of management. The idea being that if staff were more engaged, the company could be more successful, with higher levels of productivity and staff retention. Sounds great but is it really achievable? The millionaire dollar question is how do we get our staff to REALLY engage with the business? I think this focus is a healthy thing. I have been lucky enough to work for several values based businesses who do get this right – however, in my experience this has proved to be the exception rather than the norm. In my view, I think there is a part missing when talking about staff engagement. I hope this article contributes to the debate. As usual it is based on experience, so with that disclaimer, lets proceed;

Firstly, considering how to get staff engaged – there has been much work done on this, needless to say, I would summarize this as focusing on a more humane, inclusive, responsive management model / style (think Virgin or various tech companies - open holiday entitlements and variable working hours at one end). I see this as building bridges of respect, understanding, agreeing expectations, treating staff like peers, sharing a mission. It is moving away from a strictly command and control, ego based style. There are some great recognition programmes which help foster these qualities but like a husband who buys a nice present for his wife one day and then shouts and screams the next day, engagement is not a one off gesture, it must be supported by other behaviours! It needs to be CONSISTENT and CONGRUENT. (I should know, some years ago I tried the chocolates without the follow through, the increased "engagement" was rather short lived!)

Secondly, rather than ask how do we engage or retain staff engagement, possibly we need to ask another question - what are we doing that the staff are habitually not engaged or disengaging? I take a view that many staff WOULD naturally be engaged but can be switched off by authoritarian management practices or line management practices, where the well-being of the staff is not considered adequately. In response, the team pull back. I have seen this happen SO many times. I like the metaphor of Stephen Covey about the emotional bank account – is performance / effort rewarded through the culture? In various places I have worked, the staff wonder, is it really worth going the extra mile for the business? In many cases, this where staff engagement is lost or more sadly, never gained.

Could it really as simple as this? Let's look at a quote from the UK Billionaire Sir Richard Branson about the importance of a positive, engaging culture at work;

"Colleagues should take care of each other, have fun, celebrate success, learn by failure, look for reasons to praise rather than criticise, communicate freely and respect each other. "

Lastly then, I put it to you that as a leader, whether your motivation is congruence to your company values or you simply adopt these values as enlightened commercial interest, it matters little. In my view, self-awareness and emotional intelligence are key attributes needed to make a success of this new paradigm. If in doubt, ask your peers to evaluate you honestly and listen, then adjust. There are "360 degree appraisals" which can help with this. Google this if unfamiliar. Please also see start with my article on personality type with teams - https://www.linkedin.com/pulse/how-i-developed-my-leadership-team-price-pizza-liam-palmer?trk=mp-author-card

In conclusion, let's not waste our precious human capital in the workplace through practicing or allowing behaviours in our workplace which disengage our staff and ultimately hurt the organisation. Enough talking, let's do this!

1.3 Reflective practice on **Staff engagement / are we missing something?**

Key themes in this article

Accountability, positive culture, congruence.

What does this article mean to you?

What can / would you apply from this learning to your practice?

Other notes

1.4 Got problem staff? What they need is a good..?

A good talking to? Really? A challenge with a difficult staff member has made me reconsider this. Certainly in times past, I may have framed some problems as due to "problem staff" based on them exhibiting moody, difficult, bad attitude behaviours. Now, I am not so sure whether this holds true. Let me explain;

This young lady would continually contradict me in the morning meeting – seeming to score points and taking time to resist the direction I was laying down. It was difficult, I noted and thought, I wonder why she is doing that? It happened a few more times. I didn't put her in her place – not really my style but would move things on. Other team members winced. Yes, it was uncomfortable, yes I am the Home Manager, yes I need to take action but what action?

I decided to frame our chat to outline where I wanted to take the home – co-incidentally she had missed various other meetings I had given – she "was out of the loop." We sat down and this individual outlined how they operate. She shared her philosophy about work, management and tales where they felt intimidated or uncomfortable by former bosses.

Notwithstanding some unusual views, I found her to be decent and kind and true to herself. I simply said that I generally agreed and had a similar style. At the end, she said, "this has been insightful." I spoke for around 3 mins of the 1 hour. After this meeting, she was now supportive in those morning meetings, surprisingly the problematic behaviours stopped. I didn't really need to say anything but she had a need to be listened to.

In case this sounds like I am a wise sage, I am not. 10 years ago I would have talked and pressed my point. I am not wiser, simply OLDER! A lot of the time, it is really challenging to make this time, as managers we don't have it, and yet if the team member doesn't perform, how much time does it take to manage these behaviours? How much time is spent talking about them, getting advice, writing things up I wonder?

In the busyness of my day, I am going to try and keep my eyes and heart open to give that emotional support where it is really needed. I will choose to make that time. In the end I think everyone has a right to be heard and to be listened to.

1.4 Reflective practice on **Got problem staff? What they need is a good..?**

Key themes in this article

The power ad challenge of deep listening. The gift of affirmation. Focussing on our similarities rather than our differences. Give your staff unconditional positive regard (love) and accept them as they are.

What does this article mean to you?

What can / would you apply from this learning to your practice?

Other notes

1.5 Developing your team – Part 1 –fundamentals

Thank you for clicking this article - this is a real story of a real team, where we achieved a significant improvement accessing a management tool for the price of a meal for one. I have found this model is still relatively unknown, so let's start at the beginning.

For our purposes, our story starts with 2 U.S. citizens - Isabel Myers and her mother Katherine Cook Briggs. They both had a deep interest in the work of Carl Jung, the famed Swiss psychotherapist. During the second world war, when the men were sent away, women moved into industry. This mother and daughter team thought that a tool would help determine which role the new starters were best suited for. There was nothing available at the time and eventually it became their passion and life's work to produce this tool. Eventually, this led to the Myers Briggs Type Indicator (MBTI) tool that is still used today. For those who are new to this, or would enjoy a refresher on the basics, please see below;

* "The questionnaire is to help people realise their "best fit type". the personality type that will help them succeed most in life. The three original pairs of preferences in Jung's typology
are extraversion and intraversion, sensingand intuition and thinking and feeling. After studying them, Briggs Myers added a fourth
pair, judging and perceiving.

"Extraversion or Introversion: refers to where and how one directs his or her attention and energy — on people and things in the outer world, or alone in the inner world

Sensing or Intuition: refers to how one prefers to deal with information — by focusing on the basic information, or by interpreting and adding meaning

Thinking or Feeling: refers to decision making — objectively, using logic and consistency, or subjectively, considering other people and special circumstances

Judging or Perceiving: refers to how one interacts with the outer world — with a preference towards getting things decided, or for staying open to new information and options."

23

* MBTI Personality test / quoted from Wikipedia

After 30 years of research, we have a strong foundation of research to support the usefulness of the Myers Briggs Type Indicator (MBTI) tool and a new industry was born – typology within psychology.

Information on this tool can be found from their book "Gifts differing" and there are also online tests available to enable people to discover their profile / gifts. I am suggesting that 80% of the benefit of using this tool can be realised by reading this book and simply all your leadership team completing an online MBTI Inventory – though make sure it's the same one! In adopting this simplistic view, I know there will be those who may criticise this approach – to which I reply the following;

To the experts that say it is far more complex, I agree, I have just read a few books and make no claims except that in my experience being introduced to the model can be very enlightening for any team member. It can them to help them to understand and accept themselves and in turn respect their differences with colleagues too.

To the critics who say that this is an overly simplistic model and cannot possibly capture the complexity and nuances of the human personality – I agree, however, if we say that it simply helps people understand key differences of perception between themselves and others, herein for me, is the key to its value. Crucially, it also gives us a language to talk about it.

The original purpose of these pioneers was to help people identify their gifts – hence the title "Gifts differing" title quoted from Ephesians in the Good book. I think like Chinese whispers this has become distorted to become a process of categorizing a person. For me this misses the mark entirely.

We completed these tests for my team leaders and key support staff with some fascinating results. I hope that if you are not familiar with this work, it will spark an interest for you. I will share our findings in the next article. In the mean-time feel free to share your views about the use of this tool.

I hesitated to publish this first part of the article until today, one of my leadership team told me that the tipping point for her overcoming communications issues with staff was when she discovered her personality profile! Apparently, it made that much of a difference!

I dedicate this article to a former mentor Paul Brooks (Unipart / BIS / CILT). He introduced me to this model which later enabled me to embark on a major career transition – I appreciate the input - thank you!

1.5 Reflective practice on **Developing your team – Part 1 – underpinning theory**

Key themes in this article

That people's differences according to Myers Briggs are "gifts" to be developed and shared. Personal awareness. Self-knowledge. Making this info accessible at a negligible cost (consultants / trainers are a bonus but not necessary to get some benefits.)

What does this article mean to you?

What can / would you apply from this learning to your practice?

Other notes

1.6 Developing your team – Part 2 – in practice

Thank you for reading this article - it is the follow on from my previous one "Developing your team – Part 1 – fundamentals, where I outlined the advantages of using a personality profile model with your team. This can be accessed through free on-line tests and buying the book by the authors – for a very modest cost.

In this article, I want to talk about what we found when 7 key staff in my former care home took the Myers Briggs test and what that means to running a home and whether these findings could help with recruitment / succession planning.

Since the Myers Briggs model is a self-assessment with either / or questions, the following are generalisations based on observed differences in working with these individuals for just under a year. With that in mind, this is what I found;

Considering those with a T (thinking) preference as opposed to a F (feeling) preference

2 key staff - with people management responsibilities - both highly capable and respected had a "T" for thinking preference rather than "F" feeling preference in processing information. Everyone else (another 5) tested had an F preference. Co-incidentally both these staff struggled to influence their team. One quote was " I tell them what to do, I just don't understand why they don't do it". And another, " I just don't know what to do. I have told them; they just don't listen." Knowing them well, the context was that these individuals had less buy in from their colleagues and were perceived as less influential. They both did not possess the emotional calibration and sensitivity that many of their peers had but did benefit from coaching. Both were particularly strong in matters of governance and managing quality.

Considering those with an N (intuitive) preference as opposed to the S (senses) preference

Those staff with an intuitive preference or leaning were a minority and tended to think at multiple levels and conceptualise problems from different angles. The strongest ones were skilled problem solvers. The feedback was sometimes deep and insightful. Those with a sensing preference tended to have a more uniform, single dimensional approach.

Implications for managing carers

My key point here is that many carers (based on my observations) will have a "F" or feeling preference. In that sense they will instinctively prefer to be managed by someone who can relate to them in the same language (this can be learned).

Conclusions

Some staff profiles are more common / rarer than others - this was shown by Myers Briggs initial research. Judging by my research there seemed to be more people with a strong feeling preference (F) in this care home. In this work, there is a distinct need to provide compassionate care so those with that awareness seem to working in the right place!

Whilst every distinct profile will bring certain benefits however, what is most important in my view is a healthy mixture of different characters - a diverse culture which accepts the varying strengths all bring. This can be achieved through the leaders of the home being self-aware so they can understand themselves better and the value that differences bring. Thank goodness we don't need to be some sort of idealistic "perfect"!

Every combination of preferences has distinct leanings and strengths. Let's understand that and work together to create an inclusive and supportive work environment for all.

1.6 Reflective practice on **Developing your team – Part 2 – in practice**

Key themes in this article

Thinking / feeling preference- over representation of "feeling" bias people in care and the impact of this, in terms of their management. Self-knowledge, self- acceptance and self-love leads to harmony with others.

What does this article mean to you?

What can / would you apply from this learning to your practice?

Other notes

Part 2 – Masterclass in Home Leadership

Part 2 – Masterclass in Home Leadership - overview

In this Masterclass in Home Leadership, I look at some complex problems and established "challenges" within the care sector and take a contrary view to challenge some existing assumptions and paradigms.

Firstly, I start with acknowledging that being a home manager can be volatile if the operator does not have a supportive culture – I explain why this is bad for care.

Next, we look at the traditional argument that only nurses should run care homes – who leads best?

Next, we look at the biggest challenge in care – agency usage and how to move forward. There is so much misinformation in this area.

Lastly, we pull much of the material and learning together, to outline an approach that works regarding taking charge of a challenged home.

2.1 High levels of Care Home Manager attrition are hurting the UK care home industry. This is why.

As usual, please excuse the generalisations taken to keep this article brief. Thanks to those linked-in contacts that shared their stories which inspired this article. Before getting into this, we need to establish some reference points;

a) UK Care Home Context

Firstly, I want to consider the UK care home context – that our model has evolved from a hospital ward, where patients were kept in rows and kept alive through basic nursing provision. From there, the model has evolved to provide single rooms, activities, higher standards and a need for extensive documentation to evidence good care. In many care providers there has been a cultural shift to a more individual and person centred model – all these developments are welcome. The CQC has moved from inspector to more recently champion of high standards of care management leadership – "is the home well lead, safe, effective, responsive, caring" – ask the CQC guidelines. My sense is that the industry is in catch up and that our IT systems, support systems, career development ladders all need to evolve to meet this higher requirement and to be able to sustain it.

b) Unexpected consequence of home manager accountability

Like most in the industry, I welcome greater accountability and transparency and the regulators stance on this, though I would make the point that the ecosystem of the wider care home environment needs to enable the home manager to meet these high requirements. With most care businesses making extensive use of paper to record key information, there is no systemised way of managing much information, inevitably this introduces an element of risk. Also with a mix of corporate, hybrid and independent players in the sector, IT systems have evolved but not in a uniform way. Many care businesses have multiple IT systems for different functions which don't communicate with each other. This makes the task of home manager more complex than it needs to be. Herein is a temporary pressure point – whilst home managers are accountable for all that happens in their homes, in many cases their supporting systems are somewhat under-developed. This leads to a new pressure point;

c) Home Manager attrition / the problem with that

By most estimates, Home Manager attrition is running at 25- 50% across the UK care home industry. We are building more units than ever and this will continue with a sharp upturn over the next 20 years, yet home manager attrition is unusually high. I can't definitively prove the following connection, however it is possible that this partly relates to the greater expectations of the CQC, tied in with personal accountability, with an operating environment that is in catch-up.

These high levels of home manager attrition are contrary to the needs of the residents in our homes;

d) The need for those in our care

In many of the best homes I have visited, I noticed some common denominators – often key staff posts (deputy / unit manager / nurse / administrator) have been in post for 3, 5, 10 years or more. Often long serving carers, who know all the families and residents help the home feel like an extended family. This leads to my main point, that our residents at the end of their lives need stability and that stability partly comes from the continuity of the home manager; we need to reduce the home manager attrition WHILST driving up standards.

e) Impact of home manager attrition on staff and compliance

This effects the residents and crucially the residual staff team – in some homes, no-one takes the home manager seriously because they change every 6 months! This is not good for continuity of care. As the leadership changes, the whole staff team goes back to a time of building and getting established – it causes staff to feel anxious. If it happens too often it can lead staff to fully disengage, to stop trusting the company or "management". In my experience, herein lies the seeds of dysfunctional homes, with long term compliance issues -the team are unstable and there is no core residual knowledge of good practices and mature relationships with associated professionals and families. In my view, a care home does not operate in isolation but is rather a part of a complex healthcare system and a myriad of supporting professionals and the individuals and families involved in the care, it is a physical meeting point for care provision.

f) What is the true scope of the Care Home Manager role?

Herein is the crux of the matter. As a job, in most homes, it will be to be compliant with the regulators, to use the company policies as appropriate, and follow the lead of the recruiting manager. These are all a given, however, for those who have run a home, it quickly becomes apparent that the role is more than this;

The home manager is the trusted individual for those who make a decision to put their loved one in care. When that son or daughter looks the home manager in the eye, they are trusting the home manager with their mum or dad, if the home manager keeps changing, it is unnerving and does not represent the company or industry in a positive light.

The home manager is also the chief story-teller of the home, they hold the history, the context, the reputation of the home and represent it to the council, regulators, healthcare professionals, families, community at large. They act as an ambassador for care, the brand of the organisation and of the local home. Lives come into the home and at the very end we see out those final days with the family - we hold hands with those that pass as they slip away. We've shared that journey with the family, touched humanity for a moment, it's a shared knowing that our life is also finite. It matters. Community and continuity matter in this context.

It is for these additional responsibilities that the high attrition upsets the care community they serve. The industry is going through a period of change, like a storm, the home managers are bravely facing it and following the steer of the regulator and employer. There are some great examples of enlightened care operators successfully grappling with these contradictory pressures of a need for continuity, a need for a raising of standards and the challenge of high levels of attrition for care home managers. They understand the value and importance of the home managers. It can be done.

Finally, then, let's try and keep community and stabilise this crucial position in the provision of care. Let's do it for those we serve and for the courageous home managers doing a difficult job, often with good cheer. Let's do all we can to raise standards and where possible reduce home manager attrition through up-skilling, developing more robust information and home management structures to enable them to lead with confidence and skill.

Dedicated to all the skilful Care Home Managers throughout the sector. Thanks for all you do.

2.1 Reflective practice on **High levels of Care Home Manager attrit** **hurting the UK care home industry. This is why**

Key themes in this article

Cause and effect, balancing home manager accountability within the context, systems, support structures within which they work. Questioning whether managing standards through frequently moving on home managers is an effective strategy / and considering the impact on residents and teams when they are moved. Are there any other approaches which could be more effective?

What does this article mean to you?

What can / would you apply from this learning to your practice?

Other notes

2.2 Care Home Manager - who leads best- Clinical Manager or General Manager professional?

Whilst this is a very "tongue in cheek" question, in my experience this question is part of a genuine ongoing debate in UK care home leadership, where residents with nursing needs are involved. Chiefly, who leads best and in a time of increased rigour with the new regulator's framework (CQC), who has the most complete skills to get to a CQC rating of "good" or beyond? I write as a generalist who has been challenged by some former clinical colleagues claiming that only a nurse / clinical manager can "really" do it. Clearly there does need to be strong clinical leadership but is there always an advantage in that person also being the home manager? I explore below;

I greatly respect my nurse colleagues for the level of responsibility and skill they have, however, in my view, the skill of nursing is a profession in its own right, as is a Head Chef or a qualified Facility Management professional. Their jobs are organised with documentation, records, reporting protocols for legal and corporate governance and (in my experience) usually robust recruitment tools in place to ensure duties and responsibilities are clearly understood. The Home Manager has oversight of reporting, standards, audits and takes appropriate action as needed and leads by example, listening and supporting.

For my part, I have been determined to show that the distinction between the 2 disciplines is overstated. For example, no one would say that a clinical manager can't learn the theories of management science and leadership, in the same way, there is no reason why a professional and skilled general manager cannot learn the fundamentals of the clinician. In my own small way, I have tested this. After 18 months, I have finished my Diploma in Clinical Science with a Higher Merit. I am very grateful for the support of the BSY Group tutor and recommend this to my non-clinician fellow managers. Was it challenging? Yes! Understanding "peak flow, urticaria, oncogenic theory and target diastolic blood pressure" was as a foreign language to me! However, I discovered that the fundamentals are not so hard to grasp as there is a sense and structure to this body of knowledge. In fact, fear was my greatest challenge over and beyond the technical complexity.

In conclusion, I think a better question is - how can we develop clinical home managers to strengthen their general management / leadership skills and how can we develop the clinical knowledge of generalist home managers? Whilst we consider this, I believe we need to respect the complementary strengths that each approach brings. In my view, there is no "perfect" care home manager, there is just you and me, learning, growing, doing our best every day and drawing on the teams around us. Inevitably we'll all always be stronger in some things than others and after all, running a home is a team effort. I am comfortable with that.

2.2 Reflective practice on "**Care Home Manager - who leads best..Clinical Manager or General Manager professional?**

Key themes in this article

Appreciating the differences. Teamwork. Importance of upskilling and personal and professional development.

What does this article mean to you?

What can / would you apply from this learning to your practice?

Other notes

2.3 Facing the "agency problem" in UK care homes

With the minimum wage rising, and a funding gap with the publicly funded beds, care home operators are under particularly acute financial pressure, one area that could help is a sustained reduction in the use of agency staff.

Having had some useful debate with many of you very experienced and skilled home managers, I thought it may be helpful to take a fresh look at this "problem" and see if we agree what that problem is. This list is not exhaustive but instead a start;

a) Is the problem - management comfort and over-use of agency which is putting a great strain on the care industry finances? (If so, the primary solution will be about the control of the ordering of agency - approval and sign off going to higher levels of management to control / dissuade its use.)

b) Is the problem a lack of recruitment leading to an over-reliance use on agency - either through a lack of contracted hours or possibly a lack of precision about recruiting into the right areas for example? If so, putting energy into recruitment in a targeted way should solve this.

c) Is the problem about the sustainability of the location - i.e. local competition (supermarkets etc.) with wages, or perhaps a lack of transport links for staff to get to the home?

d) Is the problem a lack of managerial understanding about finance? (If so, easily fixed by a skilled mentor to a receptive home manager.)

e) Is the problem caused / aggravated by excessive sickness levels? How about staff retention levels? How about holiday management - is it well controlled?

f) How about the budget - are there sufficient hours to run adequately or is it too tight, putting undue pressure on skilled staff?

g) Is this part of a wider issue of a growing economy (reduced labour pool to draw from)? If this is a continued trend, do the options for career advancement for the carers / nurses need to be looked at (with a nod to Terry Tucker - I know this was something you have done some great work on.)

h) If the agency usage is primarily nursing - does this relate to the national shortage? Or are their wider issues in the home causing nurses not to stay? What strategies are the organisation using to address this? Are they working? Does the organisation have a culture where this level of honest communication / integrated problem solving can take place?

i) If the agency usage is primarily carers - are the wages competitive with other care homes in the area?

I guess I am trying to make the point that in my view, often agency usage per se is not the primary issue but rather a symptom of something or several things not working optimally in a specific care home ecosystem / wider industry. I am convinced that understanding the inter-relatedness of these matters is crucial.

Addressing these issues requires confident leadership from the top, balancing the quality message with cost control. In my view, it requires team spirit to share information broadly and confident managers who listen and empower teams to come up with elegant, tailored, local solutions.

I have been fortunate to meet and work with some excellent senior managers in care over the last few years. I have seen some successful agency reduction models working allied with supportive leadership, balancing quality and safety and cost. It shows that it can be done. For me, it's a call to leadership. Game on!

2.3 Reflective practice on **Facing the "agency problem" in UK care homes**

Key themes in this article

Robust critical thinking, a balanced approach, cause and effect, accountability, courage to face difficult problems.

What does this article mean to you?

What can / would you apply from this learning to your practice?

Other notes

2.4 Moving forward with the "agency problem" in UK care homes. How do we reduce reliance on agency staff? What works?

This is a follow up to my last article - Facing up to the "agency problem". My key take away was that the "agency problem" was not the problem but rather its habitual use highlighted areas in the care ecosystem not working effectively. In my view, it is a call to radical problem solving and integrated leadership within social care.

Moving on then, what can we do to reduce reliance on agency staff? This is a broad area, so please forgive the generalisations and omissions as I attempt to answer this as concisely as possible;

Opportunities for avoiding reliance on nursing agency;

In the UK, there is a nursing shortage and it's acute in certain geographical areas however, let us not use that as an excuse to avoid the hard work required to keep attracting and retaining skilful nurses. Let's consider what we can do; we can present our home or company well, have an attractive package and role. We can offer a well-managed home with a supportive management culture and room for progression. We can make our home the employer of choice for nurses in our area. We can aim to have the best managed home in the area, with the best cared for residents - right?! I accept that we are limited in the pool of talent but surely this calls for greater flexibility and persistence to differentiate our workplace from our competitors. If all we do is improve retention - that can REALLY help reduce reliance on nursing agency. Let's review our assumptions, learn from others and action, action, action!

Opportunities for avoiding reliance on carer agency workers; For many this the greatest opportunity. Let's look at "what works."

I have been involved in reducing agency reliance across several homes and consulted with many. Where there is habitual use of carer agency, providing there are not more complex issues at play (see last article), the most common cause is insufficient recruitment. In my experience this is either due to;

i) A lack of focus or recruitment process resource so the home is below the curve - carers take 4 - 12 weeks to bring on board. Recruitment needs to start before they are needed in the rota. Timing is key. (work 2 - 3 months ahead and take some measured risks on predicted occupancy.)

ii) A company imposed limit on carer hours which doesn't have enough slack to allow for leavers and the inevitable variation of occupancy. Where the tolerance around hours is too lean, with little discretion, agency reliance is far more likely. Like a bell curve, if we recruit too near the average (contracted hours), we will have too many days that are an exception - (solved by allowing a greater variation on contracted hours to cover sickness and the natural variations found in running a care home.)

Other contributory factors are;

iii) Cultural acceptance - key staff involved in the rota, and covering shifts may have got used to calling the agency when a need arises, rather than putting more energy into local efforts to cover through the team. Also, the home can get attached to certain agency workers and keep booking them (thanks DB for the anecdote!). (solved by Home Manager addressing robustly).

iv) The sickness policy is not being consistently applied. (easily remedied)

v) There is a lack of co-ordination and planning regarding holidays. (easily remedied.)

vi) There is particularly poor staff retention. Staff don't want to stay - .(retention stats will tell a story as will the body language and staff engagement on the floor. Support visits should bring this to light.)

Conclusion - let's be relentless in challenging excuses, blame and rise to the challenge by skilfully reducing reliance on agency staff, where there is potential to do so. In the meantime, agency staff and their companies are an integral part of care delivery - let 's work with them effectively, treat their staff well and appreciate the contribution they make to our services and those in our care.

2.4 Reflective practice on **Moving forward with the "agency problem" in UK care homes. How do we reduce reliance on agency staff? What works?**

Key themes in this article

Focus on taking action that will help. Understand what are the primary drivers are and where possible, take charge.

What does this article mean to you?

What can / would you apply from this learning to your practice?

Other notes

2.5 How to take charge of a challenged mid – large care home. What works?

I was emboldened to write this after speaking with other peers from different businesses - it turned out they had had used a similar solution with comparable results. As always, please excuse the generalisations needed to keep the article brief. To be clear, this is simply an outline of one effective approach.

Firstly, I need to define some of the problems and how to interpret those problems;

Why do care homes get out of control?

The reasons for this are complex – I have talked to many of you about this – here is a selection of common causes you mentioned;

It can simply be a couple of staff leave in quick succession – leading to a flurry of leavers. Then agency use goes up, morale can suffer and care quality can be effected. Since it often takes 6 – 8 weeks to recruit key staff and that leavers often only give a months' notice or less, this is common. (maybe the industry should consider giving a 2-month notice for particular positions? Food for thought

It can be ineffective leadership by a head of department, or the home manager or serious misconduct by a couple of staff.

It can be a manager with a set of skills not well suited to the needs in that particular home.

It can be a dropping of standards in one or more areas left unchallenged or staff displaying problematic behaviours that have not been successfully addressed – impacting morale and team performance.

As mentioned in the last article on care home manager attrition – a revolving door approach for managers can, over time destabilise a staff team and by implication, the home.

It can be the effect of having the wrong staff in post.

It can be support staff primarily focussing on finding fault, rather than on building competence and confidence, (not supporting.)

It can be the impact of a CQC inspection which lacks objectivity and needs to be challenged.

What is the connection between these items?

I would make 3 observations – firstly that a care home is an integrated operation – all parts are interdependent – a weakness in one area, will affect other areas and it can happen very quickly.

Secondly, in light of the above point, there may be no one party responsible for difficulties – maybe it is simply a dynamic that has been created in the home. We need to be careful about having a quick swoop in and identifying the problem before executing the solution.

Thirdly, the home is only as strong as its reputation. If people start finding fault, a sense of negativity and fear can consume the home. I am convinced that we need to emphasise operating in good faith, as a healthy team and trust each other. We need to strike a balance between positively supporting and promoting a home with dealing robustly with ineffective care and challenging poor practices.

The big picture

When you look at the list of reasons given for a home getting unstuck, it can be impossible to work out which of these overlapping points is at play, which is the primary cause? For me, this is why we need skilled managers and leaders in the sector. However, stepping away from this, my question is - what is it about care home management structures (particularly in mid to large homes) that makes this problem so common?

Key weakness in care home structures

Whilst the roles in a care home are usually well defined, in many cases, there is an under-developed (compared to industry) management structure. Secondly, communication and problem solving skills are often lacking. In my view, at the heart of this is a lack of sound management practice. Likely this is in part from the evolution of care from being a medical unit, part of a hospital and also because the nurses running many homes have received little management training. This can be remedied by more training, study and from the cross-fertilisation of skills from other management professionals moving into care.

How does this work itself out in care / why does it impact homes getting out

of control?

Where the deputy or home manager, work in a personal way (have their favourites / punish or reward those go their way) and wraps all decision making around them to bolster their position – it exposes the home to a risk of being destabilised with a number of ills;

Risk of political culture/ low morale

By working in this way, it sets a poor example to staff around – since it is not a meritocracy, politics are rife rather than a focus on good care and teamwork.

Waste of talent

By under-utilising nurses, carers, seniors, unit managers, we dis-empower them. We are wasting a great deal of talent.

Low productivity / risk

By doing this, we are usually behind in key tasks because these key people are overworked, have made themselves near "indispensable" to the operating of the home.

What can we do to address this?

Step 1 - Have a manager with empowerment, coaching and strategic management skills to assist.

Step 2 – look to develop a structure of mini-leaders under the deputy / home manager which is well defined and effectively delegates certain tasks to each of these, whilst retaining accountability with the home manager. In my experience, this is most effectively done by the following;

Step 3 – redefine job descriptions so that these roles are aligned, agreed with staff, rewarded fairly, supernumerary hours needed are all signed off and agreed. Launch in a way that the whole home supports the new positions. Conduct a transparent interview process so that a sense of fairness prevails.

Step 4 – develop this group as a cohesive team, teach them problem solving, communication skills, and coaching skills with tools to make sure they do report up necessary information so that overall control Is retained by the home manager.

In conclusion - this works simply because it utilises talent, cost effectively leverages the un-used talent in the home and liberates the home manager to oversee, direct, lead, troubleshoot rather than working in a more traditional, administration focussed approach to the role.

2.5 Reflective practice on **How to take charge of a challenged mid – large care home. What works?**

Key themes in this article

Team dynamics. The impact of individual / group behaviours. Skills lacking. Using structure / empowerment to improve performance.

What does this article mean to you?

What can / would you apply from this learning to your practice?

Other notes

Part 3 – Masterclass in Leadership Qualities

Part 3 – Masterclass in Leadership Qualities – overview

True empathy as distinct from compassion, kindness or sympathy is a very effective quality in human relations, especially useful in care. In the first article about "having a bad day..I look at some of our assumptions and judgements and how they can block connection.

Next, I look at the qualities of gratitude and appreciation. Many of us, (myself included) can be so focussed on what's ahead, we can miss the beauty right in front of us.

Next I use a story about a career change to explain the importance of flexibility and versatility to meaningful goal achievement.

Next, I look at the quality of persistence and the surprising outcomes of not being moved by circumstances.

Lastly, I look at inspiration - most effective leaders are inspired in some way and this was an example of great love leaving a legacy.

3.1 Empathy –

Having a "bad" day / an unexpected gift from a stranger in Birmingham City Centre

So here I was, let me just front this, I was having a "bad" day - mercifully it doesn't happen to me that often but today, this was it. The forces of chaos on several levels had got to me. I was fed up with my lot. It would pass, yet at that point, it was bearing heavy on me. I couldn't see a solution.

I was in Birmingham City Centre, as I walked to my car, I saw a young guy sleeping under a concrete stairwell, a filthy area and his older friend, like a father hanging around anxiously, both of European descent. I saw them tentatively, had a sense whether they were on drugs / alcohol. Were they safe I wondered? I am used to people asking for money or whatever and take a view based on each person I meet. For me, it's a fine line between getting hardened and not being a soft touch. I try to stay aware.

This gentleman wanted to show me his stuff, some basic toiletries very carefully put in a clean bag. It was a strange juxtaposition of chaos and order and he was so particular about maintaining this order in this little bag. The squalor of his living arrangements and the chaos of actually living on the street were hard to fathom. He was wanting to show me his life. I tried to empathise for a minute, he was quite lucid but broken, ashamed and slightly confused. I considered how it would be. It was heart breaking. I saw a couple of small bottles of alcohol but he wasn't under the influence. I quizzed him about it. I worried that I was giving him money to buy alcohol. In doing so, I felt bad. It felt like I was trying to get him to justify needing help. I was embarrassed of myself. He could have been my father.

I searched in my pocket, found a £10 note and gave it to him. He paused for about 5 seconds and then started crying. A grown man just started crying like that. I was pained. He was a man of dignity and self-respect, not knowing what to do, living on apples by the looks of it. My problems didn't go away that day but that gentleman gave me a reality check. I wasn't living under a concrete stairwell, I wasn't living on a diet of apples in a strange land, showing a stranger all he had in the world. I felt he was trying to get a connection and by talking to me, trying to get a sense of order in the chaos of his life right there.

He pointed at a carefully folded bit of paper with his name on and with a little broken English, explained next week, once he got to an embassy, he would be ok. He just needed to get through till then, He said he would split the money with his friend. He wanted me to know that.

Oh my friend, I did judge you for a moment, I am sorry. You are better than I and the gift you gave me was far greater than which I gave you. Thank you.

3.1 Reflective practice on **Having a "bad" day / an unexpected gift from a stranger in Birmingham City Centre.**

Key themes in this article

Empathy, other centeredness, avoiding judgements. How a giving heart often brings its own unexpected reward

What does this article mean to you?

What can / would you apply from this learning to your practice?

Other notes

3.2 Gratitude

What could be more beautiful? A time of reflection.

The inspiration for this brief share was a gentleman sharing on a video about his love for his children. In September 2015, Abdullah Kurdi lost his wife and 2 children whilst making his way to Europe as a refugee. The photo of his little boy on a beach made headlines all around the world. He was interviewed and the reporter asked him what were your children like? He said "my kids were amazing. They woke me every day to play with me. What could be more beautiful than that?"

Predictably it's a time of reflection – this space is crowded with mantras of saying "thank you", daily gratitude's, mindfulness, resolutions and plans - good things in and of themselves but I wonder whether we can still miss what is in front of us – our everyday "problems and challenges." Here I am talking about the mid-range everyday stuff of life- from work, home, partner, kids, health, money – all of which can weigh heavy at times.

I don't know about you but I have spent a lot of time looking back, lots of time forward, the challenge for me is to spend more time in today. I want to ask you to look at your life afresh, look at your "problems and challenges" and see whether there is beauty there. Could some of the wonder have got lost with the busyness and pressures in life? *NLP talks about how we associate emotions with different things, for some maybe there's no longer a feeling of joy. Let's consider some common "problems."

Are you experiencing any of the following?

Problems or dissatisfaction with your home – you have a home – hopefully warm, secure. Can that feel good?

Problems with your partner – you have a partner, been loved, taken seriously. Have a companion. Can that feel good?

Problems with your kids? You have kids one way or the other and you are a parent. How good is that?

Problems with your health? You are alive, have lived, hopefully had some good times to date with more to come. Can that feel good?

71

Problems with finances? Have you enjoyed the use of money in your life so far – cars, holidays, new clothes, homes, meals, decent food? Can that feel good?

I do not say that significant problems are not serious - they require our best attention and personally I don't subscribe to the notion that suffering is merely relative. For me, each person's suffering is personal to them and to be taken seriously with compassion, empathy, support. Every person's resources and levels of strength are different. We need to help each other where we can. I simply say that sometimes there is beauty behind your "problems", if you look a little closer.

3.2 Reflective practice on **What could be more beautiful? A time of reflection.**

Key themes in this article

The importance of gratitude, the pre-eminence of family, living in the now, family bonds.

What does this article mean to you?

What can / would you apply from this learning to your practice?

Other notes

3.3 Flexibility

How do you make a mid-life career change? I made mine at 39. Here is what I learnt;

After many good years in operations management, I came to a point where my heart just wasn't in it anymore. Deep within, I had shifted, I felt different, yet in many ways I was at the top of my own game, with lots of experience, attractive job offers, yet I wanted out, yet out to what? How do you know what to get out to?

Winding forward, I did make that transition from logistics to managing 10 departments in a wonderful private hospital in the Thames Valley. For those of you considering a significant career transition, I would love to share a formula that you could use but instead I will give you my experience and feel free to take your own meaning from it. I hope that is useful.

I had thought about moving into private healthcare, though it was undefined in my mind. It was more a direction than a plan. This changed when I went on a guided walk in central London. A nurse met me on the walk and told me about an excellent private hospital group. I got intrigued. Next, a middle management opening came up a commutable location for the same group. I gave the application ALL I could. I put in 14 hours - I precisely mapped across every experience and competence requirement. In my view, it was objectively "perfect". Excitedly I received my letter from them the next day, surely confirming my interview date? I felt like Jim Carrey in the "Yes Man" movie - here was a door opening by providence! Actually, not for long! They declined my application. It was a dead-end, yet I felt so strongly about the fit, I decided to ask for feedback. The gentleman in question was very busy running 2 hospitals. I kept calling him and eventually we talked. It was delicate. I explained it was me who had failed to clearly articulate the fit. He warmed slightly on the call, we did connect. He conceded that if our candidates don't measure up, we will invite you for interview. He offered me crumbs. I was hungry and not proud. I WANTED to move across. Crumbs are a start!

Later, I did get the call and I met this gentleman at interview. There was a fit. Half an later, I had a job offer. This was from the same guy who wrote a letter to me saying "sorry, you have not been successful". My career in private healthcare, (whatever that was) had started! I worked with some great people and will always be grateful to that business for giving me a chance.

What did I learn - firstly that my instinct was right, my skills WERE relevant and transferable. On balance, the transition worked well. Secondly, the career transition was scary. Without any sponsors in management, I was on my own. It forced me to dig very deep into my own resources and self-confidence. In conclusion, I guess if you want something enough, you make it happen. That attitude abides with me now. I read somewhere that "hope is not a strategy". I agree. I learnt that if I want it enough, MOVE OUT OF THE WAY, I am going to MAKE it happen!

3.3 Reflective practice on **How do you make a mid-life career change? I made mine aged 39. Here is what I learnt;**

Key themes in this article

Perseverance. Drive. Being indefatigable. Refusing to accept "no.". Personal confidence, accurate inventory of transferable skills. Stepping up.

What does this article mean to you?

What can / would you apply from this learning to your practice?

Other notes

3.4 Persistence

Bouncing back from redundancy / how I used linked-in to get a better position

So for those of who caught my last post, there I was in my new career in a private hospital. I had worked hard- many 7 day weeks to deepen my knowledge and create something special there. I'd improved customer service, teams were developed, absence was reduced, individuals coached, developed and promoted. IT systems implemented, physical spaces developed with skill. I was feeling confident until I got that call. "Due to funding changes...we can no longer...we want to keep our best people but.".. They were a professional outfit, supportive, decent even but.. I had a month.

When this happened to a predecessor, she broke down crying, she became critical of the business and after a couple of days didn't work her leave. That's not my way. Of course, I was shocked but for me professionalism is key. I didn't let on to colleagues until a couple of days before my month was up. I had invested myself in this work and my team. I wasn't going to change who I was due to my role coming to an end. Initially I struggled to redefine my career goals, I felt a bit lost. Within a couple of weeks, I got clear; my destination was now the sector, the values of the business, the exact make-up of the role and employer were now flexible. With this brief, I got onto google, searching for "General Manager Healthcare". This led me to create a deliberate linked-in strategy;

As I was moving from private hospital to elderly care, I felt I needed to redefine myself. I set my linked-in tagline for the role I wanted rather than what I was doing. I laid out my stall - a description of my story, why I was moving from hospital to care. Next I started deliberately connecting with my target peers - care home managers and senior support staff in the right organisations. I was transparent about why I wanted to connect - everyone who questioned my reason for connection, did later accept the connection. Then something happened, the MAGIC started at 800 connections.

Let me explain before it appears this is a magic number. It is not. It relates to having added 700 industry specific connections in the area I wanted to move into and being a second degree connection with their contacts. It starts making you VISIBLE. It increases your chances of getting "lucky". That's when the phone started to ring. I met a remarkable recruiter (D - you know who you are) who told me about this fantastic company. After a very successful year with a quality competitor, I now work there.

"Luck Is What Happens When Preparation Meets Opportunity" Seneca

To close, in case I leave the impression that this was inevitable, that it was some kind of cosmic good luck, I can honestly say the opportunity came as challenge and constraint - it was for me to create the break I wanted. Luck / fate / the universe may have played a part (if so, thanks!) but it is not something I have learned to rely on. A respected doctor and colleague from that hospital said something quite profound to me when I left - she said in time, you will see this as a step that takes you to much GREATER things. I looked in her eye, she WAS being sincere. Within a year she was absolutely right. I am really grateful to that GP for her vision and belief in me. I am also grateful to my elderly care employers giving me a chance, an opportunity to work in this sector. I LOVE working with the elderly. You know who you are - Thank you.

3.4 Reflective practice on **Bouncing back from redundancy / how I used linked-in to get a better position.**

Key themes in this article - Initiative, flexibility, using new technology, lateral thinking,

What does this article mean to you?

What can / would you apply from this learning to your practice?

Other notes

3.5 Inspiration

What inspires you to do the work you do?

On a recent overseas trip, I was asked about my motivation for my work as a care home manager – it got me thinking; without hesitation it was my maternal grand-mother, Lillian McGeehan of Portsmouth. Why did this family member exert such an positive influence – still missed keenly 25 years on? Here's some thoughts;

Lillian lived 1910 – 1989. One of 10 brothers and sisters from Plymouth – many of which worked in the houses of gentry / or on a farm – a very different time. All the family somehow fitted in a 2 up, 2 down home and were by all accounts happy. She ran away with a young (Catholic) man (big deal as she was Church of England) called Jimmy McGeehan – a kind hearted but tough talking Glaswegian.

He moved his wife to Portsmouth for a better life – he was a skilled mechanic / engineer and later worked on the famous Concorde airplane. They had 2 lovely daughters – Heather (my mum) and Gloria. He was away a lot for work and liked a drink or two when he returned – as a result, home-life was not always harmonious (this is war / post war 1940's to 1950's) yet to my Gran, he was always her hero.

By the time I got to know my Gran well – she stayed with us for a few months and we would go to visit her a few times a year. She then lived alone on the 16th floor flat of a high rise block in Southsea, Portsmouth – I guess it was a council building – all I remember was the amazing view of the Guildhall, it felt like being on top of the world. It all seemed very grand and yet I guess it was humble too.

We would go with Gran to the seafront – to the pier with the amusements, pedaloes, fish and chips, go swimming, lovely happy times with my brothers. During my teenage times (was very tall, slim and moody! – no real change then, ok not quite so slim), we would go and see gran. She was so small; in her last years she was had shrunk from around 4'11 to 4'8'. So when I was 6' 3 at 14, when she opened the door she was staring at my waist – and slowly look up, with the biggest smile you ever saw – "my boys, my boys".

Apparently I was the spitting image of her late husband Jimmy (some genetic throwback I gather.)

One particular moment summed up this lady – when getting ready for our visit, she had spent the whole day carrying these relatively huge bags back full of all the food we liked – fish fingers, Neapolitan ice cream, crisps, coke, boxes of maltesers – good times! She was exhausted but just wanted us to have a great time with her, to look after us. We watched TV on a small black and white TV in those days next to an old piano full of black and white pictures of family.

Another time, she went to her purse, got literally all her pension money (maybe £60) and said "here you go my boys. Take it" My eldest brother and I were moved beyond words – I still choke up when mentioning it. We wouldn't take it. It was such a generous and selfless, near wreck-less act – I still reflect on that often. I think it was the sheer pleasure of seeing us and joy she had with us that still remains.

Maybe that's it – that sense of unconditional love. In counselling circles, they talk about unconditional positive regard – same sort of thing. I think I have expressed a few times, in my work as a psychotherapist and I hope in my work as a care home manager. It is something that I aspire to and yet fall short more often.

In memory of my tiny gran Lillian McGeehan – thank you, we still miss you.

3.5 Reflective practice on **What inspires you to do the work you do?**

Key themes in this article

The power of personal stories, family stories. Unconditional love. The legacy of a life well lived.

What does this article mean to you?

What can / would you apply from this learning to your practice?

Other notes

Beyond Management Development for Care and Nursing Home Managers

I will be publishing an Executive Manager edition for CEO's and Company Directors and Senior Managers with unpublished material created to support the care home senior managers and owners.

There will be some leading edge behavioural change tools which can be used with staff who exhibit problematic behaviours which can negatively impact the team and home.

Watch this space – I expect it to be published by October, 2016 or earlier.

If you want to continue the dialogue;

E mail me on raisingcareandqualitystandards@gmail.com

I may not be able to respond straight away but will respond to any messages I receive.

If you want to help me with spreading the message of raising standards through developing managers, please help me by adding your review on Amazon – you will find the book listed there.

Wishing you continued success.

Liam Palmer

Printed in Great Britain
by Amazon